I0485486

Growing Your CIO Career

How CIOs Can Work With The Entire Company In Order To Be Successful

"Practical, proven techniques that will help you to make your CIO career long and successful"

Dr. Jim Anderson

Recent Books By The Author

Product Management

- Product Management Secrets: Techniques For Product Managers To Boost Product Sales And Increase Customer Satisfaction

- Customer Lessons For Product Managers: Techniques For Product Managers To Better Understand What Their Customers Really Want

Public Speaking

- Secrets To Organizing A Speech For Maximum Impact: How to put together a speech that will capture and hold your audience's attention

- How To Become A Better Speaker By Changing How You Speak: Change techniques that will transform a speech into a memorable event

CIO Skills

- What CIOs Need To Know About Working With Partners: Techniques For CIOs To Use In Order To Be Able To Successfully Work With Partners

- How CIOs Can Make Innovation Happen: Tips And Techniques For CIOs To Use In Order To Make Innovation Happen In Their IT Department

IT Manager Skills

- How IT Managers Can Make Innovation Happen: Tips And Techniques For IT Managers To Use In Order To Make Innovation Happen In Their Teams

- Secrets Of Effective Leadership For IT Managers: Tips And Techniques That IT Managers Can Use In Order To Develop Leadership Skills

Negotiating

- Learn How To Package Trades In Your Next Negotiation

- Learn How To Signal In Your Next Negotiation: How To Develop The Skill Of Effective Signaling In A Negotiation In Order To Get The Best Possible Outcome

Miscellaneous

- The Internet-Enabled Successful School District Superintendent: How To Use The Internet To Boost Parental Involvement In Your Schools

- Power Distribution Unit (PDU) Secrets: What Everyone Who Works In A Data Center Needs To Know!

- **Note**: See a complete list of books by Dr. Jim Anderson at the back of this book.

Published by

Blue Elephant Consulting

Tampa, Florida

Printed in the United States of America

Library of Congress Control Number: 2015916790

ISBN-13: 978-1517688585
ISBN-10: 1517688582

Warning – Disclaimer

The purpose of this book is to educate and entertain. This book does not promise or guarantee that anyone following the ideas, tips, suggestions, techniques or strategies will be successful. The author, publisher and distributor(s) shall have neither liability nor responsibility to anyone with respect to any loss or damage caused, or alleged to be caused, directly or indirectly by the information contained in this book.

Acknowledgements

Any book like this one is the result of years of real-world work experience. In my over 25 years of working for 7 different firms, I have met countless fantastic people and I've been mentored by some truly exceptional ones. Although I've probably forgotten some of the people who made me the person that I am today, here is my attempt to finally give them the recognition that they so truly deserve:

- Thomas P. Anderson
- Art Puett
- Bobbi Marshall
- Bob Boggs

Dr. Jim Anderson

This book is dedicated to my wife Lori. None of this would have been possible without her love and support.

Thanks for the best 24 years of my life (so far)...!

Speaking.   Negotiating.   Managing.   Marketing.

Table Of Contents

CIOs Don't Have Time To Grow Their Careers!

Just becoming your company's CIO is not enough. Once you reach this lofty point, you are going to have to take on the responsibility of growing your career so that it can truly become the challenging opportunity that you've been seeking. The good news is that this can be done. The bad news is that it's never easy.

As CIO you are going to have to form relationships in order to the approvals for your major projects. Who should you spend your time with: the CEO or the CFO? It may not matter that much because it turns out that we all work in sales in some form or another. As the CIO you are going to have to make sure that you fully understand how your company's sales organization works so that you can support them.

The role of CIO is changing. It is taking on more and more of an appearance of being a Strategic Execution Officer role and you are going to have to adapt to this. In order to accomplish all of this you may end up having to appear to be two-faced at times. If this doesn't happen, then it may be time for your company to do like a lot of other companies are doing and say goodbye to the CIO position.

The key to being a successful CIO is making sure that you have a good understanding of just exactly what a CIO does. This means that you have to take a look at what CIOs do and then learn from them. In order to be a successful CIO, you may decide that you need an MBA. There are a lot of different ways to go about getting this degree – which one is the right one for you?

It is my hope that after having read this book you will be aware of the additional job that you've taken on as CIO – managing your career. Do this correctly and your CIO career will last a long time…!

For more information on what it takes to be a successful CIO, check out my blog, The Accidental Successful CIO, at:

www.TheAccidentalSuccessfulCIO.com

Good luck!

-   Dr. Jim Anderson

About The Author

I must confess that I never set out to be a CIO. When I went to school, I studied Computer Science and thought that I'd get a nice job programming and that would be that. Well, at least part of that plan worked out!

My first job was working for Boeing on their F/A-18 fighter jet program. I spent my days programming fighter jet software in assembly language and I loved it. The U.S. government decided to save some money and went looking for other countries to sell this plane to. This put me into an unfamiliar role: I started to meet with foreign military officials and I ended up having to manage groups of engineers who were working on international projects.

Time moved on and so did I. I found myself working for Siemens, the big German telecommunications company. They were making phone switches and selling them to the seven U.S. phone companies. The problem was that the switches were too complicated. Customers couldn't tell the difference between one complicated phone switch from another complicated phone switch. Once again I found myself working with the sales and marketing teams to find ways to make the great technology that the engineers had developed understandable to both internal and external customers.

I've spent over 25 years working as an senior IT professional for both big companies and startups. This has given me an opportunity to learn what it takes to manage and IT department in ways that allow it to maximize its output while becoming a valuable part of the overall company.

I now live in Tampa Florida where I spend my time managing my consulting business, Blue Elephant Consulting, teaching college courses at the University of South Florida, and traveling to work with companies like yours to share the knowledge that I have about how to create and manage successful IT departments.

I'm always available to answer questions and I can be reached at:

Dr. Jim Anderson
Blue Elephant Consulting
Email: jim@BlueElephantConsulting.com
Facebook: http://goo.gl/1TVoK
Web: http://www.BlueElephantConsulting.com/

"Unforgettable communication skills that will set your ideas free…"

Create IT Departments That Are Productive And A Valuable Asset To The Rest Of The Company !

Dr. Jim Anderson is available to provide training and coaching on the topics that are the most important to people who have to manage IT departments: how can I build a productive IT department (and keep it together) while at the same time providing the rest of the company with the IT services that they need?

Dr. Anderson believes that in order to both learn and remember what he says, speakers need to laugh. Each one of his speeches is full of fun and humor so that what he says "sticks" with everyone.

Dr. Anderson's CIO SkillsTraining Includes:

1. How to identify and attract the right type of IT workers to your IT department.
2. How to build relationships with the company's senior management in order to get the support that you need?
3. How to stay on top of changing technology and security issues so that you never get surprised?

Dr. Jim Anderson works with over 100 customers per year. To invite Dr. Anderson to work with you, contact him at:

Phone: 813-418-6970 or
Email: jim@BlueElephantConsulting.com

Blue
Elephant
Consulting

Speaking Negotiating Managing Marketing

12

Chapter 1

Who Should A CIO's BFF Be:
The CEO or The CFO?

Chapter 1: Who Should A CIO's BFF Be: The CEO or The CFO?

The times they are changing. Let's take a moment and have a talk about one of a CIO's key survival skills: the ability to successfully negotiate office politics. Specifically, if you could only have **one best friend**, who should it be: the CEO or the CFO?

Changes In The Workplace

The workplace that a CIO works in looks nothing like it did as little as 10 years ago. The changes that have happened have reshaped the boundaries of power. The CEO used to be the **rock star** who acted as a visionary leader. Think of Bill Gates, Tom Siebel, and Larry Ellison. However, the corporate scandals that rocked the business world at the start of the new millennium (i.e. Worldcom, Enron, etc.) have created the need for a change at the top.

Philip Tulimieri and Moshe Banai have taken a look at the changes that have been taking place in the C-suites of major firms. They believe that a new focus on **ensuring accountability** by the senior executives, especially the CEO, plus the arrival of new regulations such as the Sarbanes-Oxley Act have changed who investors want to have running the company.

In the past, CFO were generally **in the shadows of the CEOs** – simply acting as mangers of the company's money and trying to make sure that the company didn't do anything too wild that they couldn't pay for. This is all changing now.

The Arrival Of Co-Leaders Of A Company

In today's corporate world, the balance of power is shifting. No longer is the CEO the only person running the show. Instead, the CFO is now playing a larger role – sorta a **co-leader** if you will.

The roles of a CEO and CFO are still different. A CEO has the responsibility of always being **positive** and working to move the company forward at all times. The CFO, on the other hand, is responsible for making sure that the company approaches every situation with **caution** and does its best to minimize the risk that it is being exposed to.

Tulimieri and Banai have made the interesting discovery that the rise of the CFO has meant that the role of the **Chief Operating Officer (COO)** has started to decline. The CIO is also responsible for this – that automation of much of a firm's back office operations has reduced the need for the COO.

What's A CIO To Do?

CIOs need to navigate these new corporate political waters very carefully. Yes, the CEO is still an important ally to have on your side; however, no longer is this enough – now you also have to **be on good terms with the CFO**.

One of the biggest challenges going forward will be keep both leaders happy. It's important to realize that there will be **disagreements** between the CEO and CFO and that's when the CIO needs to be most careful.

The challenge for any CIO is on which relationship should the most time should be spent. This will be different for every company. However, the CIO has the opportunity to show a great deal of value by **facilitating communication** between these two executives.

Final Thoughts

A CIO who can provide the information that a CEO needs in order to drive the company forward while at the same time providing the information that the CFO needs in order to measure the risk, will be seen as being **valuable**.

The arrival of the CFO at the top of the company's decision making structure means that being able to **measure the financial value** of every IT project will become even more critical. The world changes and CIOs need to make sure that they pick their corporate friends very carefully!

CIOs who can survive in the new world of company leadership and who can find a way to make friends with both the CEO and CFO will be better at finding ways to apply IT to enable the rest of the company to grow quicker, move faster, and do more.

Chapter 2

It Turns Out That CIOs Really Work In Sales

Chapter 2: It Turns Out That CIOs Really Work In Sales

It turns out that a company's **#1 salesperson** is their CIO. They may not go on sales calls, have an assigned quota, or even be up-to-date on the company's latest product pricing plans, but at the end of the day the CIO is the one who drives (or drives away) the most sales.

Why Software Can Kill A Sale

In our modern times, almost every company has a fancy **Customer Relationship Management (CRM)** application that they use to keep track of who their customers are and what they've either sold to them or promised to them. You might be thinking that when you become CIO your only obligation to the sales team will be to keep the CRM application up and running. Turns out you'd be wrong.

Life has changed a great deal over the last few years and the relationship between IT and a company's sales teams has changed right along with it. This has been necessary because in today's global economy a company's **customers want to be involved** in the creation of your products. Your CRM software is going to be standing in the way of this.

What's Wrong With The CRM Software That You Are Using

Customers are shrinking the number of vendors that they are willing to do business with in order to make their supply chains more efficient. This means that they are going to want to be able to work with your company in order to **see their product suggestion ideas start to show up in your products**. In a nutshell, they want you to change to better meet their needs.

Your CRM software is not only not going to be able to do this, but it's actually going to be standing in your way once you are the CIO. At its core, your CRM software is an internal application that is designed to do one thing and do it well: it helps your salespeople to track their customers and it allows sales managers to track their salespeople. Note the **absence of customers** in all of this.

CRM software does a great job of managing your internal sales systems. However what you are going to need as CIO is a way to manage your customer relationships – the dialogue that is going on outside of your company's walls.

All Of Those Other Customer Conversations That Need To Be Managed

The reason that this is now part of what a CIO has to do is because the way that the company's sales teams interact with their customers is now very **heavily dependent** on the IT department. Let me count the ways:

- **Social Networking:** Twitter, Facebook, LinkedIn, you name it and Sales is probably using it to reach out and connect with their customers.

- **Wikis**: Gone are the days of static product documentation, say hello to dynamic documents that can be updated by customers based on their own experience with your product.

- **Product / Customer Portals**: who wants to search through a company web site to find the information about just the products that they have bought? The era of customized portals that eliminate the clutter and just provide the information that a customer really wants has arrived.

- **Teleconferencing**: sure voice calls were nice, but now we've got web-cams and shared whiteboarding tools that turn a dry short meeting into a dynamic interactive session.

- **Co-Design Tools:** the old way of designing a new product or service and then taking it to the customer is out the door. Now customers can participate in the design process and what is produced is right the first time.

What All Of This Means For You

All too often CIOs see the Sales department as not being part of the company's IT infrastructure. This is wrong, wrong, wrong. A much better way to look at things is to think of the CIO as being **a key part** of the company's sales team.

When you become CIO you are going to be (partially) responsible for the **success of the sales team**. One of your most critical tasks will be to find ways to use the company's IT resources to help the sales teams develop deeper and better relationships with their customers.

The old way of just making sure that the company's CRM system is up and running will no longer cut it. You are going to have to do some homework and find out the **multiple different ways** that your salespeople are connecting with their customers. Once you know this, you'll be better positioned to leverage your IT department to help them become selling machines.

Chapter 3

The 5 Secret Characteristics Of A Truly Great CIO

Chapter 3: The 5 Secret Characteristics Of A Truly Great CIO

In all honesty, there are a lot of people who become CIO who really **should never have been promoted to that position**. There are too many IT folks who are only good at ensuring that company IT resources are properly and efficiently used. I'm not saying that this is a bad thing, only that this kind of skill set is not what it takes to be a really good CIO. Do you know what it takes to be a good CIO?

Direction

When we start to think about what kind of qualities that a CIO needs to have in order to do his or her job correctly, hopefully the quality of being able to generate and communicate **a clear sense of direction to others** is one of the first ones that comes to mind.

Businesses never stand still – either they are moving forward or they are falling behind. A CIO does not lead the business, that's the CEO's job, but the CIO is responsible for showing the IT department **the way that they are going to move forward**. This involves creating two important things: goals and a vision.

Inspiration

Just knowing where you want the IT department to go to is not enough. As CIO you are also going to have to be able to get everyone in the department to get off their behinds and start to **move in the correct direction**.

It turns out that everyone is already moving, it's just that they are moving in a whole bunch of different directions. A CIO that is able to inspire an IT department will be able to get everyone to **line up** and work towards making progress in the same direction.

Team Building

A great CIO realizes that although some people can be fantastic individual contributors, that's not enough for an IT department to be successful. What is needed is for people to stop working by themselves and for them to **start working as a team**.

Although this may sound rather intuitive, it turns out that it runs counter to what most IT workers want to do. We all want to be recognized for our **individual accomplishments** and when you are working as part of a team, this can be much harder to do.

A great CIO has the ability to make people want to work as a part of a team because they realize that that is the only way that **big challenges can be met**. A great CIO will take the time to acknowledge the accomplishments of a team, but at the same time he / she has the ability to look within the team and understand who contributed what to the outcome.

Lead By Example

All too often, what the CIO says is not what he / she ends up **doing**. If the CIO is still throwing lavish brainstorming sessions for upper management when budgets get tight, then this will not go unnoticed.

A CIO who physically shows up when a big cut-over is being performed, or works a weekend when the rest of the team is struggling to meet a big deadline will earn the **respect of the department**.

Acceptance

Great CIOs realize that they have been appointed to manage the IT department by a higher authority, but they are not truly a leader until their people **accept** them as such. This is the kind of acceptance that can't be commanded, it has to be earned.

In the case of a CIO, it will be a combination of things that cause a department to accept their leadership. Specifically, their staff will be looking for proof that the CIO is up to the job. It will depend on the CIO's performance during a few fire drills, a demonstration of how the CIO handles a situation in which he / she has clearly made a mistake – do they admit it or do they blame someone else, and finally **it will take time**.

What All Of This Means To You

Potentially anyone can become a CIO. Only a very few of us can become a **great CIO**. The difference between the two types of CIOs comes down to one word – leadership.

We all like to talk about just what it takes to be a great leader, but what we all too often forget is that it's not just about the CIO, but rather about the IT staff – is this a person that **they want to be led by?**

A great CIO can be clearly recognized by **five distinct characteristics**: the ability to provide clear direction, the ability to inspire, the ability to build successful teams, commitment, and finally, being accepted as the leader by the rest of the IT department. Now you know what you have to do, go out and do it.

Chapter 4

It Takes A Strategic Execution Officer To Get Anything Done Around Here

Chapter 4: It Takes A Strategic Execution Officer To Get Anything Done Around Here

We all dream of the day that we will get the nod to become CIO — finally we will have arrived. Or will we have? Take just a moment and think about all of those major projects that you've see during your career that started out with a bang and ended up **failing** and going away with a whimper. When you are CIO, things are going be different and that's because you won't just be the CIO, you'll also be the company's Strategic Execution Officer.

What Have I Signed Up For?

Business processes are like pit-bulls: they really don't like change and if you try to change them, they are probably going to bit you really, really hard. This is one of the reasons that so many major company initiatives **fail** — nobody really wants to go to the effort to change.

What's been missing for far too long has been a **Strategic Execution Officer** and since so many of today's major projects involve the IT side of the house, who better to assume this role than the CIO?

In your future role as your company's CIO / Strategic Execution Officer you will not only be responsible for making sure that the new IT systems go in on time, but also that the company's processes and the behaviors of the staff are changed so that the new way of doing business **actually gets implemented**.

Sound challenging? It does to me. That's why we need to reach out to researchers Dr. Jeanne Ross and Dr. Peter Weill who have taken the time to look into what **four things** a Strategic Execution Officer needs to do. Let's see what they recommend.

Create & Manage IT Systems Used For Strategic Initiatives

A CIO will tend to look at a given project and search for ways to get it successfully implemented. A Strategic Execution Officer realizes that in order for the company to be successful, the **core processes** that allow the company to operate smoothly and efficiently need to be digitized.

This means not just one IT project, but potentially **several** need to be done in such a way that they support the company as it is today and as it will be tomorrow. Key components of this type of solution include a single well-managed database, a standardized development system that allows the creation of different applications to easily talk to each other, and a solid communications network so that workers can access the data and applications that they need from just about anywhere.

Become A Leader In How The Company Does IT Governance

The CIO / Strategic Execution Officer is the one person in the company who is best situated to **see it all**. This means that you are going to have to take an active role in the company's IT governance process.

You are going to have to be able to make some hard calls when it comes to identifying what the company's IT priorities are. On top of this, you will have to be able to **communicate to others in the firm** what the different trade-offs are to each decision.

Make Business Units Actually Use Digitized Business Processes

Time to play Mr. Tough-Guy here. As Strategic Execution Officer you are going to have to show up and make each of the company's business units **start to use** the new digitized business processes once the implementation is done. This is not going to be easy to do.

We all know how this plays out: a project goes in and then half of the company finds a way to get their jobs done without using the new system because they don't want to be bothered to learn how the new system works. You must not allow this to happen. If you have to **take away the systems that are allowing them to work around the new system**, then so be it.

Create Both Structures And Initiatives That Make The Company Change

Making the entire IT organization ultimately report to the Strategic Execution Officer solves the problem of how to motive the IT staff to follow through on a company-wide change. In firms that have multiple CIOs, this is one way to quickly solve a lot of **common structural problems**.

Getting the business unit leaders to sign up and agree to use the results of a multi-year IT project can be tricky. Identifying and removing real and perceived obstacles is one way to go about doing this. Another is **taking the time to talk** with each business unit leader in order to make sure that they understand why the change is happening and how they will benefit from it.

What All Of This Means For You

Becoming the CIO of your firm will be a **major accomplishment** in your IT career. However, far too many of us have become CIOs only to eventually fail at implementing some major company-wide project.

The reason that so many of these projects fail is because the company lacked a Strategic Execution Officer to see the project through from start to finish. This is a role that you are going to have to be willing to **step up and play**.

As the Strategic Execution Officer you will be responsible for coordinating projects that span the entire company. Your ability to be successful at doing this won't rest so much on your technical skills as they will rest on your ability to **motivate the business unit heads to participate** in both the project and its final results. Good luck!

Chapter 5

Two-Faced CIOs:
Dr. Jekyll, Meet Mr. Hyde

Chapter 5: Two-Faced CIOs: Dr. Jekyll, Meet Mr. Hyde

Just imagine the day that you become CIO: you'll be able to shed all of those past associations and friendships that have gotten you to this exalted position and finally you'll be able to focus on what really matters: forging strong links with your company's **senior management**. Well, sure, if you don't really need to get anything done...

The Best CIOs Are Two-Faced

It turns out that you're not going to be able to get rid of everyone that you've known in the past — they're still an important part of how you are going to be a successful CIO. The secret to being a good CIO that you need to find a way to **simultaneously live in two completely different worlds**: you're going to need to lead the IT team and you're going to need to be a member of the senior management team.

If you had to pick which one of these sides of your CIO personality was more important, I'd bet that you'd be torn: the old people that you've know or the shiny new people that you want to know? It turns out that your relationship with your IT team is **probably more important**— they are the ones who are going to allow you to actually get things accomplished.

Building An IT Team

Although building a strong and smoothly working IT team will be one of your most critical IT tasks, it's also going to be one of your **most difficult challenges**. As CIO you are going to have step up and establish ground rules for how you want your IT teams to:

- Communicate
- Make decisions
- Handle conflicts
- Evaluate Performance

In order to get the highest level of performance out of your team, you are going to have to work with them to make some **very basic agreements** about what goals they should be pursuing, who has what roles, and the processes that will be used to achieve these goals.

Playing With The Big Boys

If all that a CIO had to do was to lead the IT team, the job would be much easier. I mean after all, that's the world that you've always been living in, right? The other face of a CIO looks towards the company's other **senior management**. Just as when the CIO is working with his / her IT team, there are a completely separate set of goals associated with this team:

- Finding ways to share information
- Building a common company culture
- Creating strategy
- Working together to solve problems
- Aligning the company's organization in order to realize its strategy

Much of your success in this area will rest on your ability to **focus** on what's really important: how the overall business is doing.

What All Of This Means For You

When you become CIO, you will also become a **split-personality**. One part of you will be focused on creating and maintaining successful IT teams. The other part of you will be trying to work with the other senior executives at your company.

The one nice thing about these dual roles is that you'll know that you are **being successful** when the same thing happens in both of your dual roles. When everyone feels that they are required to share their thoughts on what's happening outside of their area, then you know that they really care and that you've done your job as CIO.

Chapter 6

CIO's In The Wild: A Field Report

Chapter 6: CIO's In The Wild: A Field Report

One of life's great mysteries is "just exactly what do CIOs do" I'm pretty sure that we all think that we know what they do, but do we **REALLY** know? In order to prepare you for your future job as a CIO, I have undertaken a dangerous field study in order to observe the wild CIO in their natural habitat and I'm now prepared to make my report back to you. Listen and learn.

The Subject

Our subject in this case was Mr. Lindsey Jarrell who is currently the CIO of **BayCare Health System**. BayCare is a community-based health care system in the Tampa Bay, Florida, area. They connect patients to a complete range of services through their not-for-profit hospitals, outpatient and imaging facilities, and other regional services that reach beyond the Bay area.

These observations were made as part of my attending a healthcare conference that was being held in the Tampa area. Lindsey had been invited to give a talk about how BayCare has been **using IT as a part of its operations**.

Overall Knowledge

In order to judge how a CIO is doing his job, you have to take a careful look at just **what he says**. This is truly a case where words may speak even louder than actions.

Lindsey showed that a CIO needs to know about **more than just IT issues**. The key to being a successful CIO appears to have a good understanding of where the company is trying to go and how the IT department can help it get there:

- **IT Vision:** The goal of BayCare's IT department is to understand how physicians think.

- **Relationships:** The CIO has to have a good relationship with the Chief Medical Information Officer (CMIO). This required Lindsey to get over his need to always be in control.

- **Extra Knowledge:** Things that the BayCare CIO needs to know about that are not IT related include how doctors work and a lot about vendor contracts.

- **Who Owns Quality?:** A company's quality project is not an IT project, instead it is a company-wide transformation project.

- **Deep Knowledge:** Lindsey was able to quote off the top of his head the incoming call volume that his help desk was currently fielding.

IT Projects

IT is all about **projects**: we start them, we run them, and hopefully the company is made better by them in the end. It was clear that Lindsey had spent a lot of time trying to find the best way to do IT projects and here's what he had to say about that:

- **Where?:** Lindsey was able to admit some of the functionality of the large-scale project did not have to be located in the IT department.

- **Keeping The Right Focus:** He believes that his project teams needed to be out in the field in front of the doctors. One of the reasons for this is that inside of BayCare they have a completely different focus: they deal with an in-patient environment whereas doctors are focused on people who come to their offices (out-patient care).

- **Dates:** He believes that for large IT projects you need to avoid announcing a "go live" date until AFTER you are either weeks or months into the project and have a good understanding of what it's really going to take.

- **Project Management:** The CIO came to understand that vendors really only care about getting to "live" (which is when they get paid). Realizing this, Lindsey hired his own project manager who is responsible for keeping track of the "big picture" for his projects.

What All Of This Means For You

This kind of observation of a real, live CIO is exactly the kind of information that **you need to be considering** as your career moves you closer and closer to the day that you'll be named CIO. Hopefully my field notes have provided you with some insights into what a CIO really does.

Of special note should be the fact that Lindsey didn't spend any time talking about servers, operating systems, development tools, networking, or security issues. These are all part-and-parcel of what an IT department deals with on a daily basis, but Lindsey realized that these are **internal issues** that nobody else cares about. CIO's need to focus on what the rest of the business wants and keep the IT stuff inside the IT department.

Chapter 7

Is It Time To Say Goodbye To The CIO?

Chapter 7: Is It Time To Say Goodbye To The CIO?

So you want to be a CIO someday. Great. However, there may be a bit of a problem with your goal — the position of CIO **may be going away**. In fact, in about 10 years or so (is that when you are planning on seizing the reigns of IT control?) the position may look completely different from how it looks today. Hmm, a moving target. Maybe we should talk with some current CIOs to find out just what's going on here...

Do CIOs Still Need To Have Business Skills?

Over at CIO Insight magazine they just got done doing their annual survey of CIOs. The results were, to say the least, eye-opening. The answer to the most asked question about the need for CIOs to have business skills is still a definite **YES**.

Current CIOs report that they are acting as much as business leaders as technology leaders. The days in which a CIO could lose himself / herself in the world of IT and be left alone appear to be **long gone**.

There is a bit of a double standard going one here however. CIOs are reporting that although they are being asked to implement programs that will result in fundamental business improvements, the position of CIO is still being pushed back to the **second tier** of senior management.

What Skills Do CIOs Need To Have Today?

With all of this talk of business skills, won't CIOs need to have solid technical knowledge going forward? The answer appears to be yes, but. CIOs are saying that **the job skills that they use most** include finance, business process modeling, written and spoken communications, and just a bit of some sales and marketing skills. I sure didn't see servers, bandwidth, application security, or API knowledge anywhere on that list.

In fact, CIOs are reporting that the folks who are currently getting hired into IT positions have, can you believe it, **even less business knowledge** than people did just two years ago. This is quickly going to cause a problem: there are going to be very few qualified candidates to become CIO over the next few years. Can anyone say "opportunity"?

Skills That CIO Wannabes Need To Be Working On

You might be asking yourself, so **what skills do I need** to be working on to take advantage of the need for business savvy CIO candidates that will be coming in the future?

The list is actually fairly short. To start with, you need to have very good public speaking skills and the leadership skills that will be required to implement what you talk about. A detailed understanding of the business that you are working for (like how they **REALLY make their money**) and a solid understanding of corporate finance.

There is, of course, more to this list. Once you've mastered the basics, then you'll have to **keep adding skills**. Today's CIOs report that you'll also need to know how to master the strategic use of information, how to lead enterprise-wide changes, perform business model innovation, and improve business processes.

What All Of This Means For You

The report from today's CIOs is not all good. It sure looks like CIOs are currently being treated as **second-class citizens in the**

C-suite. However, as we all know, IT is not going away and it sure is not getting any less important. I'm thinking that CIOs are actually going to become more important over time.

CIOs are reporting that although business skills are becoming an even more important part of the set of tools that a CIO needs to have, fewer and fewer IT hires are coming with these skills. Clearly this is **opening the door** for those who dream of someday becoming the CIO.

Although it looks like you might have a shot at the **top spot**, it's not going to be handed to you. You're going to have to work at it. We've laid out the skills that you need to develop. Now go out there and get ready for the day that they call your name to become the firm's next CIO...!

Chapter 8

CIOs In Crisis:
Do We Have A Problem Here?

Chapter 8: CIOs In Crisis: Do We Have A Problem Here?

You and I both know that a well-run IT department is what can make one company **more successful than its competitors**. That must mean that the IT department is important, and therefore the CIO must also be important, right? If that's true, then why are some of the really big companies like News Corp, Harrah's, ConocoPhillips, etc. getting rid of their CIO and then choosing to not replace him / her? What are they thinking?

What's The Problem Here?

If firms feel comfortable getting rid of their head of IT (the CIO) and not replacing that person, then clearly there must be **a crisis here**. It sure looks like today's CIOs have not done a good job of advertising just how valuable they are to the rest of the company's executive leadership team.

This is pretty easy to understand. However, there's a problem with this explanation. You would think that all of the upper management positions would be faced with this same challenge of conveying their value to the company. However, it seems like the CIO is the only position that companies feel comfortable leaving either open or in the hands of a less senior member of staff. You can't say the same for operations, finance, human resources, etc.

What Could We Do To Solve This Problem?

Arthur Langer has been researching this issue and he believes that the problem that IT has is that we're **lacking support**. If we worked in accounting, then we'd all be CPAs and everyone would agree on the way that things needed to be done.

IT has no equivalent accreditation system. Langer points out that the field of IT is lacking any sort of **professional body** that could provide its stamp of approval for how an IT department is run or what goals it chooses to focus on. Although such an organization may be a long way off, in the near term IT at least needs to do a better job of getting the message across to the CEO about IT actually does.

Langer makes a good point when he states that he believes that there is no question that CEOs value what an IT department does. It's just that what we do is so far removed from what he or she understands, that CEOs really have **no clear idea how to manage their IT resources**.

Ultimately, this is what is currently missing: **an IT best practices organization** that can provide CEOs with this kind of management guidance. Sure we've got the ITIL standards, but those are far too detailed. What's missing is that top-level "here's how you run an IT department" type of guidance.

What All Of This Means For You

Even though you may not yet be a CIO, you need to start thinking about how you are going to effectively deal with this issue. The last thing that you want to have happen is for you to finally become the CIO only to lose your job because the job itself was seen as being **not all that important**.

As CIO what you are going to have to do is 1) do a good job of running your IT department, and 2) do a good job of educating your CEO on how to manage his / her IT assets. This means that you're going to have to do **a lot of different tasks**: create IT best practices for your company, collect industry research and show it to your CEO, create management guides to instruct your CEO on what you need him / her to do for IT. Congratulations – when you become CIO, you also become a teacher!

Although this may seem like it would take up a lot of your precious CIO time that could be spent forging strategy and harnessing new technology, think again. Teaching your CEO how to manage the CIO and showing how to use IT to make the company more successful just might be **the best thing that you've ever done** – it could even save your job!

Chapter 9

Just Exactly What Did The Big CIOs Do Last Year?

Chapter 9: Just Exactly What Did The Big CIOs Do Last Year?

To say that last year was a rough year, might be the understatement of the decade. Every business seemed to be taking it on the nose and anytime you opened the paper or turned on the TV, it just seemed as though the bad news kept on coming. What's interesting for all of you who dream of someday becoming a CIO, is that the best CIOs didn't allow all of the bad news to discourage them – they still made progress...

Yes, I believe that we all know what the right thing to do is. However, sticking to our guns when it seems like the rest of the world is falling apart all around us **is what separates the good CIOs from the not-so-good ones**. What does it take to keep moving forward? Most of the best CIOs all agree that even in bad times an IT department should be an externally directed force that is focused on growth, customers, and creating market-facing leadership

The Best CIOs Still Made Progress

Amazingly enough, a global recession can be good for business. It shakes out the weaker companies and primes customers to start buying again once things pick up again. Bob Evans has been talking with some of the CIOs for the biggest global firms and he's found out that **they've been quite busy**, despite the global recession. Here are some examples:

- **Liu Zhixuan, CIO of China's Shenzhen Airlines:** Liu has been working on what he calls a **"service-chain integration" project** for the airline. Once it's in place, this IT solution will offer an end-to-end view of not just the airline's business processes but it will also allow customers to be segmented. As an additional value to the airline, this project will automatically reset the outcomes of some of business processes based on a customer's status.

- **Kim Tac Keuk, CIO of LG Electronics: :** Since my current cell phone is made by LG, I'm always interested in what they are up to. During the past year Kim has lead their efforts to implement a **global single-instance Oracle ERP system**. Anyone who has been involved in one of these projects knows what a bear they can be even when they aren't global in nature. This project started off by requiring an 18-month effort to map, integrate, and optimize 440 business processes across LG's 83 subsidiaries. What I liked best about this accomplishment is that it gave the IT department intimate knowledge about how the company does business. Kim believes that it is important also because he says that in his company IT teams must be masters of all processes across the enterprise.

- **Tania Nossa head of IT for Alcoa Brazil: :** Making Aluminum requires a lot of raw material and energy. Trying to create a successful company to do this is difficult enough even when you aren't in the middle of the Amazon rainforest. Tania spent last year **working to extend and upgrading the company's connectivity**. This might not seem like such a big deal, until you consider that it means running LAN cables down into mines in the Amazon rainforest – then you start to appreciate what he's been able to accomplish.

- **Alan Matula, CIO of Royal Dutch Shell: :** One of the things that many want-to-be CIOs forget is that very little of what a CIO does has anything to do with technology. For example, Alan spent part of his time last year **signing over $4B in outsourcing contracts**. Clearly he's going to have a big job in the upcoming year managing and keeping track of each of those contacts.

Oh, and during the same year he implemented one of the world's largest unified communications solutions. That makes for a full year!

What All Of This Means For You

It's all too easy to get distracted by what we read in the newspaper and see on TV. This past year was an excellent example of how bad news can flood our minds and **distract us from what we really should be doing**.

As Bob's research has shown, the best CIOs didn't allow a global recession to stop them from **moving forward**. Sure it may have impacted their budgets and slowed their projects down, but they still made progress.

Learning by example is how one can become a great CIO. Let what these CIOs accomplished this year serve as an example for you on how to keep your eye on the prize as you work towards becoming a great CIO.

Chapter 10

Does A CIO Need To Have An MBA Or Is There Another Way?

Chapter 10: Does A CIO Need To Have An MBA Or Is There Another Way?

If you want to be a CIOs, then there's no need for me to tell you that we are living in troubling times We are always trying to do two things: hold on to our jobs and find ways to move up the corporate ladder. One of the best ways to do both of these, or so we have been told, is to **go out and get an MBA**. Well that's all great and fine if you've got four or five years to burn, don't need to do anything else at night, oh and have a big chunk of cash sitting around that you had no other plans for. Maybe it's time to look for a better way to accomplish what we're trying to do…

Say Hello To The Alternative To The MBA

Before you decide to either quit your current job and go back to school in order to get an MBA (really, really expensive) or start going to night school to get an MBA (just really expensive), maybe you should take a moment and **consider all of your options**. Maybe what you really want is a specialized Master's degree.

Yeah, yeah – I know what you are thinking. We've all been drinking the "get an MBA" Kool-Aid for so long that it's hard to imagine doing anything else. However, depending on what you want to do with your life, **this might actually be a better solution for you.**

If having spent time in your job has gotten you interested in the business side of the company, then getting an advanced business degree of some sort is probably a good idea. However, one of the things that keeps us from doing this is often **the time involved to get the degree.**

The Appeal Of Specializing

Business schools are starting to get the message. They are beginning to offer more and more specialized business programs that are only 12 months long. In the 2008-2009 school year **there were 645 programs offered**. This is up from the 614 programs that had been offered just two years earlier.

What these types of degrees offer are parts of the typical MBA curriculum, but they are often more technical in nature and generally **spend less time on general management skills**.

Here in lies the rub: these types of specialty business degrees are not designed to get you promoted to eventually become the CIO. Rather what they are designed to do is to sharpen your business skills in a narrow area and **make you more valuable to the company in that niche**.

This type of continuing education especially appeals to **new IT managers**: those who don't have the five years of work experience that most MBA programs require for entrance. No matter if this is your case, or if you've just found some part of the business job that you are really drawn to, a narrowly focused master's degree might be just the ticket for you.

What To Do With Your New Degree

Ok, so let's say that you bite the bullet and run off and skip the MBA and instead get a very focused master's degree in marketing, finance, or some other business discipline. **What then?**

It turns out that taking this path, might feel like the right thing for you to do, but as they like to say on TV, **your results may vary**. Since specialty master's degrees are not as well-known as

MBA's you're going to have to deal with some lack of recognition issues.

Although it may change in the future, right now **MBA students still seem to get the best deal** when it comes to getting the economic benefits from going through the effort of getting an advanced degree. The people who design the GMAT test that everyone takes to get admitted to graduate programs are reporting that MBA students are saying that they get a 73% increase in salary after graduating while students with specialty master's degrees are only reporting a 26% increase.

What All Of This Means For You

In the end **the decision rests with you**. We all know that continuing our education is an important thing for every up-and-coming member of the IT department to do. Going back to school almost seems like a no-brainer until you realize that you need to spend some time thinking about just what you want to get out of doing so.

A specialty master's degree offers IT workers who have been working for less than five years or who found one particular part of the job most interesting with a new option. By investing 12 months of study, they can walk away with both another degree as well as **a deep understanding** of one area of business.

The value of taking this educational route will really depend on the career that you want for yourself. If you believe that when you become CIO that you'll need to be able to have a detailed understanding of how your business works, then a specialty master's degree **might be the right way to go for you!**

Chapter 11

Is Life Easier If You Are A CIO Who Works For The U.S. Government?

Chapter 11: Is Life Easier If You Are A CIO Who Works For The U.S. Government?

You want to become a CIO. You probably want to become a CIO in the private sector – you know, those companies that have owners or stockholders that they always have to work to keep happy. Why haven't you spent any time thinking about becoming a CIO who works for **the biggest employer out there**: the U.S. Federal government?

Big Changes Coming

The U.S. Federal government (the one that runs the country, not the states) employs **over 300 CIOs** that manage all of the different parts of the operation. You would think that federal CIOs would have it easier: I mean they don't really have to worry about keeping shareholders happy or anything like that, do they?

You need to keep in mind that although a federal CIO doesn't have to worry about the same things as a private sector CIO, they have a whole bunch of **different issues** that occupy their time. One big issue is that every four years they may have a completely new boss what with the presidential elections and all that.

As the U.S. experiences the effects of the global recession just like everyone else, federal CIOs are feeling the pressure to show that their IT departments can deliver **a solid return on investment (ROI)** .

It's becoming pretty clear that **there is a lot of IT funding for the things that you would expect a federal CIO to be working on**: things like wireless projects and public safety projects. However, this doesn't leave a lot left over for all the other things that an IT department is supposed to be working on,

What Are A Federal CIO's Biggest Priorities?

One of the key ways to tell if being a federal CIO is any different from being a private sector CIO is by taking a look at what's on **their list of projects**. Federal CIOs always have to be nimble enough to adjust to a new administration's priorities which may differ from the last administration's. This can cause a big change in what the IT department spends their time working on.

Right now the federal CIOs are reporting that **the key programs** that their departments are working on include:

- Virtualization
- Data Center Consolidation
- Green IT
- Federal Enterprise Architecture
- Continuous Process Improvement
- Business Intelligence
- IPv6 Transformation
- Application Performance Management

How Are They Going To Be Successful?

So if you were a federal CIO right now, how would you go about pulling off all of these initiatives while dealing with the tightest budgets in years? As you might be able to guess, **there is no one magic answer to this question**.

In a survey done by InformationWeek magazine, 21% of federal CIOs said that they were using Lean Six Sigma. 29% reported that they were using ITIL. Even within the military **there was no one way to go**: the U.S. Army is using Lean Six Sigma while the Navy is planning on using ITIL.

What All Of This Means For You

In your future, there is actually a good chance that you might at some time **become a federal CIO** – there sure are a lot of them out there. You might have thought that this was an easy route to take – no pressure from owners / shareholders. Think again.

Federal CIOs have to deal with **a great deal of upheaval** in their upper management structure on a cyclic basis. On top of that even during difficult economic times they need to find ways to push forward on important IT programs that will transform their organizations.

If you do become a federal CIO, I sure hope that you like change. You'll have your own set of issues to worry about, **but at least things won't be boring!**

Chapter 12

Is Your CIO Resume iPhone Ready?

Chapter 12: Is Your CIO Resume iPhone Ready?

When you go hunting for your next IT job (and it may be sooner than later), **will your resume be up to the job?** Come to think of it, when was the last time you dusted off and updated your resume? Do you still have that quaint "objective statement" or "career goal" hanging out at the top? If so, you may be in for a shock – that's not going to be the best use of resume real estate when it's being reviewed on the hiring manager's iPhone…

The Need For A New Resume

Parting is such sweet sorrow… or so the classic line goes. Look, when did you first create your resume? A while ago? Even if it was only a couple of years ago, **the world has changed dramatically since then** and it's time that you (and your resume) kept up with it. It's time to say goodbye to your old style resume.

About that "objective statement" up at the top – **ditch it**. The next company that will be hiring you really doesn't care about what you are looking for. Instead, they are facing pain right now and they are looking for someone whom they can hire to come in and make that pain go away. That's what really matters.

This means that we're going to have to make some changes to your current resume. **Prepare to get out the sharp knife.**

Length

How long is too long? How long is too short? This rule of thumb has not changed even in the 21st Century – **a resume should be two pages max.** In fact, it's really only the first 25% that you can count on a hiring manager reading so that's where you've got to really shine.

If you've had some amazing IT department experiences that you think would really help your case, then feel free to include them – **as an addendum**. This extra stuff can be anywhere from 4-12 pages long; however, remember that there is no guarantee that anyone is going to read it.

Skills

Are you the world's best Cobol / Fortran / Java programmer? Drop it. Look, you're going for a IT leadership job and it's really your finance and people management skills that are going to get you the job – **not your programming chops**. Use your limited resume real estate to explain how your leadership skills have made your past departments successful.

Skip The History Lesson

A resume is designed to tell your next employer about how you'll perform in the workplace. This means that pretty much anything that does not have to do with the workplace **should be dropped**. This list will include civic accomplishments, professional associations that you belong to, charity work, etc. Use the freed up space to provide more details about your most recent job and how it relates to the job that you are applying for.

Say No To Descriptions, Yes To Accomplishments

I must confess that this has been a mistake that I've made in the past and I found it hard to stop doing it. Instead of providing your work biography by listing every single job you've ever had, use the space instead to **list your accomplishments**. Ultimately this is what your future employer really cares about. Don't worry about all of those "title only" promotions that you've gotten over the years, instead just focus on the teams that you've managed and the challenges that you've mastered.

What All Of This Means For You

Everyone has a resume. However, not everyone has a resume that will work for them. In this day and age of everyone having too much to do and too little time to do it in, you're going to need to shape your resume **to be scanned quickly on your future boss' iPhone** as he/she dashes off to their next meeting.

What this means is that you're going to have to **cut to the bone** and get rid of everything that doesn't pertain to how you would do in your next position. Detailing what you've accomplished in your most recent leadership positions is what that iPhone scanning hiring manager is going to be looking for.

Take the time to craft a new resume that is tailored to read quickly in digital form and **you'll be one step ahead of everyone else** who is applying for the same job. If you make it easy for them to see why you are the perfect fit for the job, then you've just shown them why you're the type of IT talent that they need to hire...

It's from the forge of failure that the steel of success is formed.

Hard Work Does Not Guarantee Success, But Success Does Not Happen Without Hard Work.

- Dr. Jim Anderson

Create IT Departments That Are Productive And A Valuable Asset To The Rest Of The Company !

Dr. Jim Anderson is available to provide training and coaching on the topics that are the most important to people who have to manage IT departments: how can I build a productive IT department (and keep it together) while at the same time providing the rest of the company with the IT services that they need?

Dr. Anderson believes that in order to both learn and remember what he says, speakers need to laugh. Each one of his speeches is full of fun and humor so that what he says "sticks" with everyone.

Dr. Anderson's CIO Skills Training Includes:

1. How to identify and attract the right type of IT workers to your IT department.
2. How to build relationships with the company's senior management in order to get the support that you need?
3. How to stay on top of changing technology and security issues so that you never get surprised?

Dr. Jim Anderson works with over 100 customers per year. To invite Dr. Anderson to work with you, contact him at:

Phone: 813-418-6970 or
Email: jim@BlueElephantConsulting.com

12

Photo Credits:

Cover - By: Craig Sunter
https://www.flickr.com/photos/16210667@N02/

Chapter 1 - By: Public.Resource.Org
https://www.flickr.com/photos/publicresourceorg/

Chapter 2 – By: Ged Carroll
https://www.flickr.com/photos/renaissancechambara/

Chapter 3 – By: Jim Forest
https://www.flickr.com/photos/jimforest/

Chapter 4 – By: Sean MacEntee
https://www.flickr.com/photos/smemon/

Chapter 5 – By: Andrew Steele
https://www.flickr.com/photos/enderst07/

Chapter 6 – By: radaris.com
radaris.com

Chapter 7 – By: www.huffingtonpost.com
www.huffingtonpost.com

Chapter 8 – By: Taber Andrew Bain

https://www.flickr.com/photos/andrewbain/

Chapter 9 – By: studio curve

https://www.flickr.com/photos/studiocurve/

Chapter 10 – By: opensource.com

https://www.flickr.com/photos/opensourceway/

Chapter 11 – By: Doug Kerr

https://www.flickr.com/photos/dougtone/

Chapter 12 – By: Kenny Louie

https://www.flickr.com/photos/kwl/

Other Books By
The Author

Product Management

- Product Management Secrets: Techniques For Product Managers To Boost Product Sales And Increase Customer Satisfaction

- Product Development Lessons For Product Managers: How Product Managers Can Create Successful Products

- Customer Lessons For Product Managers: Techniques For Product Managers To Better Understand What Their Customers Really Want

- Product Failure Lessons For Product Managers: Examples Of Products That Have Failed For Product Managers To Learn From

- Communication Skills For Product Managers: The Communication Skills That Product Managers Need To Know How To Use In Order To Have A Successful Product

- How To Have A Successful Product Manager Career: The Things That You Need To Be Doing TODAY In Order To Have A Successful Product Manager Career

- Product Manager Product Success: How to keep your product on track and make it become a success

Public Speaking

- Secrets To Organizing A Speech For Maximum Impact: How to put together a speech that will capture and hold your audience's attention

- How To Become A Better Speaker By Changing How You Speak: Change techniques that will transform a speech into a memorable event

- How To Give A Great Presentation: Presentation techniques that will transform a speech into a memorable event

- How To Rehearse In Order To Give The Perfect Speech: How to effectively rehearse your next speech to that your message be remembered forever!

- Secrets To Creating The Perfect Speech: How to create a speech that will make your message be remembered forever!

- Secrets To Organizing The Perfect Speech: How to organize the best speech of your life!

- Secrets To Planning The Perfect Speech: How to plan to give the best speech of your life

- How To Show What You Mean During A Presentation: How to use visual techniques to transform a speech into a memorable event

CIO Skills

- What CIOs Need To Know About Working With Partners: Techniques For CIOs To Use In Order To Be Able To Successfully Work With Partners

- Critical CIO Management Skills: Decision Making Skills That Every CIO Needs To Have In Order To Be Able To Make The Right Choices

- How CIOs Can Make Innovation Happen: Tips And Techniques For CIOs To Use In Order To Make Innovation Happen In Their IT Department

- CIO Communication Skills Secrets: Tips And Techniques For CIOs To Use In Order To Become Better Communicators

- Managing Your CIO Career: Steps That CIOs Have To Take In Order To Have A Long And Successful Career

- CIO Business Skills: How CIOs can work effectively with the rest of the company!

IT Manager Skills

- How IT Managers Can Make Innovation Happen: Tips And Techniques For IT Managers To Use In Order To Make Innovation Happen In Their Teams

- Staffing Skills IT Managers Must Have: Tips And Techniques That IT Managers Can Use In Order To Correctly Staff Their Teams

- Secrets Of Effective Leadership For IT Managers: Tips And Techniques That IT Managers Can Use In Order To Develop Leadership Skills

- IT Manager Career Secrets: Tips And Techniques That IT Managers Can Use In Order To Have A Successful Career

- IT Manager Budgeting Skills: How IT Managers Can Request, Manage, Use, And Track Their Funding

Negotiating

- Learn How To Signal In Your Next Negotiation: How To Develop The Skill Of Effective Signaling In A Negotiation In Order To Get The Best Possible Outcome

- Learn The Skill Of Exploring In A Negotiation: How To Develop The Skill Of Exploring What Is Possible In A Negotiation In Order To Reach The Best Possible Deal

- Learn How To Argue In Your Next Negotiation: How To Develop The Skill Of Effective Arguing In A Negotiation In Order To Get The Best Possible Outcome

- How To Open Your Next Negotiation: How To Start A Negotiation In Order To Get The Best Possible Outcome

- Preparing For Your Next Negotiation: What You Need To Do BEFORE A Negotiation Starts In Order To Get The Best Possible Deal

- Learn How To Package Trades In Your Next Negotiation

Miscellaneous

- The Internet-Enabled Successful School District Superintendent: How To Use The Internet To Boost Parental Involvement In Your Schools

- Power Distribution Unit (PDU) Secrets: What Everyone Who Works In A Data Center Needs To Know!

- Making The Jump: How To Land Your Dream Job When You Get Out Of College!

How To Use The Internet To Create Successful Students And Involved Parents

How CIOs Can Work With The Entire Company In Order To Be Successful

> This book has been written with one goal in mind – to show you how you can successfully grow your CIO career. It's not easy being a CIO so we're going to show you what you need to be doing in order to make your career a success!
>
> **Let's Make Your CIO Career A Success!**

What You'll Find Inside:

- **WHO SHOULD A CIO'S BFF BE: THE CEO OR THE CFO?**

- **THE 5 SECRET CHARACTERISTICS OF A TRULY GREAT CIO**

- **CIOS IN CRISIS: DO WE HAVE A PROBLEM HERE?**

- **IS YOUR CIO RESUME IPHONE READY?**

Dr. Jim Anderson brings his 25 years of real-world experience to this book. He's been a senior IT executive at some of the world's largest firms. He's going to show you what you need to do (and not do!) in order to make your CIO career a success!

www.ingramcontent.com/pod-product-compliance
Lightning Source LLC
Chambersburg PA
CBHW070931180526
45168CB00003B/1033